Eliza's House

A Play

Brendan Murray

A Samuel French Acting Edition

SAMUEL FRENCH

FOUNDED 1830

SAMUELFRENCH-LONDON.CO.UK
SAMUELFRENCH.COM

ELIZA'S HOUSE

First performed in The Studio, The Royal Exchange Theatre,
Manchester, on 6th June 2001, with the following cast:

Man and **Boy**	Simeon Andrews
Girl	Kathryn Drysdale
Woman	Christine Mackie

Directed by Wils Wilson
Designed by Louise Ann Wilson
Lighting designed by Natasha Chivers
Sound designed by Peter George Rice
Music directed by Olly Fox

CHARACTERS

Man, Maurice Metcalf, mid/late 40's; and **Boy**, Maurice aged
10-13
Woman, Eliza Metcalf, née Madden, Maurice's mother, late
30's
Girl, Beth O'Rourke, about 12

The action of the play takes place in a room in a council house

Time—the present and, in flashback, the 1960s

MUSIC

The music used in the original production of **ELIZA'S
HOUSE** was the Bruch Violin Concerto No.1 in G minor.

For my sister, Kath,
Because, because, because, because ...

For their patience, help, advice and encouragement my thanks go to: my friends David, Laura, Barbara, John, Andrew, Richard, Pia and Noel; Crispin and Lyn at DSL; Amanda, Sarah-Jane, Sarah and Matthew Lloyd at RET; Matthew B at the end of a phone and Louise and Wils at the end of their tether.

Brendan Murray

ELIZA'S HOUSE

A room in a council house. The present. Afternoon

A flight of stairs with a Yale-locked walk-in cupboard beneath it leads off US. There are two doors into the room, one from the kitchen and one from the front door; through the latter doorway a hallstand can be seen. The décor of the room dates from the 1960s or earlier. Objects in the room include: a sideboard with a pair of brass candlesticks on it, an easy chair and a record player with records (none of them with an outer sleeve)

When the play begins the room is lit by a dim afternoon light

There is the sound of the front door being opened slowly, then closed

A Man, balding, aged between forty and fifty, appears in the hall doorway, silhouetted there. He doesn't put on the light but comes into the room and looks round, picking up this and that; unsure, puzzled even. He opens the record player and looks at the record on the turntable

Violin music plays

A Woman in her thirties, forty years ago, comes down the stairs, her arms full of bedding. She heads for the kitchen

Woman Can you hear this, Maurice? Are you listening? This could be you. If you practise. This could be you.

The Woman exits into the kitchen

The Man stands lost for a moment in another time. His mobile phone rings; the music snaps off. We're back in the here and now

Man (*answering the phone*) Hallo? Yeah. ... Yeah, I know. ... Yeah. ... No, but I'm getting it. ... A couple of days — tops. ... Yeah. ... Yeah, I will. ... I know, yeah ... (*The phone call over, he goes to the cupboard and tries the door. It's locked*)

The Man exits up the stairs

There is a pause, then the sound of the front door being opened again

This is swiftly followed by the entrance of a Girl of about twelve. She wears a hooded jacket, obviously not hers, with the hood up

The Girl puts on the light, goes to the record player and turns it on. The same violin music as before plays from the record player. The Girl takes down her hood; closes her eyes and takes a deep breath. Then she opens her eyes, goes over and looks at the brass candlesticks

The Girl exits into the kitchen

The Man appears, tentatively, on the stairs

Mum..? (*He comes further into the room*) Mum ... ? (*He moves towards the kitchen door*) Mum, is that ——?

The Girl enters with a tin of metal polish (Duraglit) and a cloth. Seeing the Man, she screams and drops the metal polish

The Man gasps and steps back in turn. The Girl pulls up her hood. They stand looking at one another. Pause

What the ...?
Girl Who ...?

Beat

Man Who the …?
Girl What …?

Beat. Then they both speak at once

Man Look, I don't know who you are or what you're doing here but if you clear off now I won't call the police or anything so you be a good kid and we won't say anything more about it.

Girl If you've come here looking for money and stuff there isn't any and Mrs Metcalf's not even here so if you leave whatever you've taken and just go I won't tell anyone you even broke in.

Man What?
Girl What?

Pause. The Girl switches the music off

Man This is private property, you know.
Girl I know.
Man Someone lives here.
Girl I know, so how …?
Man Often break into other people's homes, do you?
Girl I didn't break in, you did.
Man I didn't break in: I've got a key.
Girl So have I.
Man What?
Girl (*producing a key*) See.
Man But this is my mother's house.
Girl Your mother? (*Beat*) Oh!
Man Yeah. So now what have you got to say for yourself?
Girl You mean ——
Man Changed your tune, now, haven't you?
Girl Mrs Metcalf?
Man What?
Girl Mrs Metcalf's your mum?
Man How …?
Girl So you must be her son.

Man Who ...?

Girl If Mrs Metcalf's your mum then you're her son!

Man (*after a beat*) Yeah, well, that's the way it usually works.

Girl Oh! I thought you were a burglar.

Man A burglar? I'm not a ——

Girl (*retrieving the metal polish*) She's not here, you know.

Man No, I know she's not.

Girl She's in the hospital.

Man I know.

Girl Course you do or you wouldn't be here, would you?

Man How d'you mean?

Girl I mean that's why you're here. That's why you've come.

Man How do you know why ...?

Girl My nan said they were sending for you.

Man Your nan?

Girl Yeah.

Man What's your nan got to do with it?

Girl She said they said, when she went to the hospital.

Man Yeah, well, she's right: they did. Send.

Girl Have you been yet?

Man Where?

Girl To the hospital, you know, to see your ... Mrs Metcalf.

Man Oh. No. No, not yet. Look ——

Girl Why not?

Man Well, I just got here, didn't I?

Girl What, just now?

Man Yeah. Look ——

Girl God! You must be absolutely ——

Man What?

Girl I mean I bet you'd like a cup of tea.

Man Why?

Girl Coming all that way.

Man Well ...

Girl From New Zealand.

Man Where?

Girl New Zealand: where you live.

The Girl exits, leaving the metal polish

Man (*to himself*) New Zealand?

We can hear the kettle being filled

> *The Woman enters from the kitchen, forty years ago, with a pile of clean sheets, and exits upstairs*

Girl (*off*) We did it in Geography. And Australia. Are there really more sheep there than there people?
Man (*back in the now*) Look, I don't know why you think ——

> *The Girl enters from the kitchen*

Girl Would you rather have tea or coffee?
Man What?
Girl Only there's only powdered milk and some people don't like it in tea, do they?
Man No?
Girl My dad can't stand it; says it tastes like paint, you know.
Man What are you talking about?
Girl My dad and powdered milk.
Man I mean, what's going on?
Girl How do you mean?
Man I mean what are you doing?
Girl Making the tea.
Man No, I mean ... Who are you? What are you doing here? Here: in my mother's house.
Girl Oh, I see.
Man Well?
Girl This is where I come.

The Man looks puzzled

> To wait for my dad.

The Man looks yet more puzzled

Till he gets home from work.

Man Your dad?

Girl Yeah, he doesn't like me being on my own.

Man Oh.

Girl No, so I come here to sit with your ... with Mrs Metcalf — till he gets home, cos sometimes he's late, you know; depends.

Man What about your mum?

Girl Ran off with the milkman.

Man What?

Girl That's what my dad says.

Man Oh.

Girl It was when I was a baby. I don't remember her. It's all right.

Man Is it?

Girl My dad says one woman's enough for any man to have to deal with.

Man Right. Well, haven't you got any friends you could go to?

Girl I just live next door, see.

Man Oh.

Girl Yeah.

Man With your dad.

Girl Yeah.

Man And your nan.

Girl No. (*Beat*) Not my nan. Just my dad.

Man But I thought ——

Girl There's the kettle.

The Girl exits

Man (*after a pause; realizing something*) But ——

Girl (*off*) Tea or coffee?

Man What? Oh ... Coffee, yeah — if it's powdered milk.

Pause. The Man hangs his jacket by the foot of the stairs then pauses by the record player

The Lights cross-fade to a state that indicates the past

The Woman enters down the stairs, forty years ago. She wears a pearl necklace. She watches the Man for a moment

The Man becomes his younger self, the Boy

Woman (*of the record player*) What do you reckon?
Boy Is it ours?
Woman Course it's ours; whose do you think it is?
Boy I don't know.
Woman Well?
Boy Yeah, it's good. Yeah. Where d'you get it?
Woman There was a card in the paper shop. One of those houses off Stockport Road. You know, by the hospital. Selling everything, they were: cooker, dining suite, television. Emigrating. New Zealand.
Boy It's not new, then?
Woman No, it's not new, but it's not old; they only got it last year, apparently. And he brought it round. Big car. Nice fella. Very smart.
Boy Did it cost?
Woman Enough. But there's records with it, see.
Boy Can we put one on?
Woman I don't see why not. He did show me ...
Boy I know.
Woman Do you?
Boy We've got one at school.
Woman Go on, then.
Boy (*picking up a record*) There's no cover.
Woman No, I know.
Boy None of 'em have got any covers.

During the following, the Boy puts the record on the player

Woman They were in a box, he said, but the dog got it or something.
Boy Did you buy 'em?
Woman 'Em, Maurice? What's 'em?
Boy Them. Did you buy them?
Woman Well, I didn't pinch them, did I? No, he let me have them for nothing. There's a full set, he said. Are you sure that thing's supposed to be like that?
Boy Yeah, and then you do this and it all works.

The Boy presses "Play" and the record drops into place. They watch as the arm swings over and down.The music — the same violin music — plays but at the wrong speed; far too fast. The Boy does a manic impression of a violinist

Woman Well, that's not right, is it? I thought you knew how to do this.

Boy I do! It's on the wrong speed, that's all

The Boy changes the speed setting; the music slows

Woman That's better! (*She sets to work on the candlesticks with the Duraglit*) Do you know who this is?

Boy No.

Woman It's a very famous violinist. I heard him once on the radio when I was a girl.

Boy Is it all like this?

Woman Years ago now. And I pretended it was me. Me, playing like: "Eliza Madden, the famous virtuoso"! And I kept hearing it in my head, you know, the music from the radio; like when you listen to a shell and hear the sea ... So when it was Christmas I asked my dad if I could have one, a violin; have lessons, learn and that.

Boy What did he say?

Woman (*smiling*) Oh, I can't remember.

Boy But did he get you one?

Woman What do *you* think?

Boy Why not?

Woman Well, because violins cost a lot of money, never mind lessons. And your granddad was out of work, wasn't he? All the time I was growing up, really. There was no money for violins. No money for decent clothes half the time.

Boy What about when you got older?

Woman Well, then I was working, wasn't I, and there was no time. And then there was the war and then ... But whenever I heard the violin played proper ... (*Beat*) Anyway, now we can listen whenever we want.

Boy And can we get some other records?
Woman Would you like to be able to play like this?
Boy The violin?
Woman Of course we'd have to get you one.
Boy I thought they cost loads of money.
Woman Perhaps when you go to the Grammar ... What do you reckon?
Boy I haven't even passed yet.
Woman No, but you will.
Boy (*picking up the metal polish and smelling it*) Haven't even done the exam.
Woman (*fingering her pearls*) I know. And don't be smelling that. It's not for smelling. You can do the hall mirror if you're so keen.
Boy (*putting the polish down*) Jimmy O'Rourke's getting a bike.
Woman Is he?
Boy A racer.
Woman Well, he'll not be going to the Grammar.
Boy A Raleigh.
Woman And Jimmy O'Rourke hasn't got these lovely records to listen to, has he?
Boy Do we have to listen to 'em now?
Woman *Them*, Maurice; it's *them*. How do you stop it then?

The Boy presses "Eject" and the music stops. They watch the record player clunk to a halt

Ha! (*Heading for the kitchen*) Fish fingers for tea.
Boy Yeah!

His mother gone, the Boy continues to look at the record player

The Lights return to their previous state, indicating the present

Girl (*off*) Do you take sugar?
Man (*back in the now*) What?

The Girl enters

Girl Sugar?
Man Oh, yeah. Yeah: one and a bit.
Girl (*heading back to the kitchen*) Like your mum.

The Girl exits

Man (*after a beat*) And that's another thing.
Girl (*off*) What?
Man You come here to sit with my mother.
Girl (*off*) After school, yeah.
Man So you won't be on your own.
Girl (*off*) Till my dad gets home.
Man But she's not here, is she?

The Girl enters with a cup of coffee on a saucer

Girl I know she's not.
Man She's in hospital.
Girl I know.
Man So you are on your own.
Girl (*after a beat*) You're here.
Man Well, today, yes, but ...
Girl (*handing the cup to the Man*) There you go.
Man (*taking it*) Oh, yeah. Right. (*Pause*) You cold or something?
Girl How d'you mean?
Man I mean that jacket.
Girl What about it?
Man Is it yours?
Girl Yeah.
Man And what are you doing with the hood up?
Girl (*after a beat*) Like you say, I'm cold.
Man (*after a moment*) What's your name, then?
Girl Beth.
Man That short for Elizabeth?
Girl No.
Man It is, though, i'n't it?
Girl No.

Man I mean sometimes.
Girl Well, it isn't!
Man All right. (*Pause*) So when does your dad get here?
Girl Like I say, it depends; you know, what time he finishes.
Man Oh.
Girl Is it all right?
Man What?
Girl Your coffee.
Man Oh, yeah. It's fine. (*He drinks*) Very nice. The china cups ...

The Woman enters, forty years ago, with a box, some china cups identical to that used by the Man, and some newspaper. During the following, she wraps each cup in newspaper and puts it in the box

Girl There's only one.
Man One? Used to be a whole set.
Girl Would you rather have a mug?
Man Cups, saucers, plates.
Girl Only I thought with you being a visitor ——
Man I'm not a visitor.
Girl You're visiting though, aren't you?
Man I'm not a visitor.
Girl (*after a pause*) The Queen drinks out of cups like that.
Man My mother tell you that?
Girl If you hold it up to the light, you can see through it.

The Man holds up his saucer; the Woman, forty years ago, holds up a cup and decides not to wrap it up and put it away but to keep it

Man Yeah.
Girl That's how you can tell it's the real thing.
Man Wonder what happened to the rest.

The Woman exits with the box. Pause

So this is what you usually do, is it?
Girl When?

Man When you come round.
Girl To wait for my dad?
Man You make the coffee, do you?
Girl Sometimes. Or sometimes I run errands if your … If Mrs Metcalf wants anything; or we do the brass, you know, the candlesticks.
Man She has you doing that?
Girl I don't mind.
Man And the hall mirror.
Girl I like the smell. Of the stuff.
Man (*picking up the metal polish*) Duraglit. (*He smells it*)
Girl And don't be smelling that; it's not for smelling.

He looks at her

That's what she says: your … Mrs Metcalf.

Pause. The Man puts the Duraglit down

Mostly though, we just sit.
Man And what?
Girl Talk.
Man About?
Girl Anything: school; the weather; you.
Man She talks about me?
Girl All the time.
Man What does … ? I mean what has she …
Girl Oh, you know, she tells me what you said in your last letter; how your concerts are going and everything.
Man Concerts?
Girl Your violin concerts.
Man She ——
Girl And then we listen to your records.

Again the Man looks puzzled

This is my favourite.

The Girl plays the record again. Music fills the room

The Woman enters, forty years ago, counting money. Then she removes her necklace and looks at it. She considers for a moment then exits

Man So ... She's told you all about me.
Girl Yeah.
Man That I'm a violinist.
Girl Yeah.
Man And that I live in New Zealand.
Girl Yeah.
Man Right.
Girl And that you're called Yehudi.
Man (*choking on his coffee*) You what?
Girl Yehudi Menuhin.
Man She told you that?
Girl I know it's a secret.
Man I'll say.
Girl And I know it's not your real name. Just what you call yourself to play the violin and make your records and that.
Man Right.
Girl Which is your favourite?
Man Oh, I like this one, too.
Girl Sometimes I pretend — you know, when we're listening to the music — sometimes I pretend it's me.
Man Yeah?
Girl It must be fantastic. To play like this.
Man Yeah.
Girl Like ... where the yellow meets the sea.
Man You what?
Girl You're dead lucky.
Man Yeah. Dead.

The Man's mobile phone rings. He looks at it

Girl Do you want me to ——?

Man No, it's all right. I'll go upstairs.

The Man exits up the stairs

The Girl turns the volume up

The Lights cross-fade to a dreamlike setting

Transfixed by the music, transported, transfigured, the Girl mimes playing the violin like a virtuoso. The sound of the sea mixes with the music. She takes down her hood and dances, wildly, freely

The Man returns, goes straight to the record player and turns it off

The Lights return to the "present" state

Man When did you say your dad'll be here?
Girl What? (*She pulls up her hood*) Oh. Not yet.
Man He's taking his time, isn't he?
Girl Like I say ——
Man Yeah, I know: it depends.
Girl You don't have to wait.
Man What for?
Girl I mean if you want to get to the hospital, you can just go. You don't have to mind about me: I'll be all right.
Man Right. Yeah. (*Pause*) There's something I have to do first.
Girl What is it?
Man I just need to find something.
Girl What?
Man A key. You can help me if you like.
Girl Key?
Man (*looking around*) Yes, for this cupboard.
Girl (*after a beat*) Is it locked, then?
Man You don't know where it is, do you?
Girl What?

Man The key. You don't know where it is? It used to be upstairs on her dressing-table but I've been upstairs twice now and I can't see it. (*He continues his search during the following*)

Girl What do you want it for anyway?

Man I want to open the cupboard, don't I?

Girl (*after a beat*) Have you finished your coffee?

Man No. I thought you were going to help me.

Pause. She helps him look, but very half-heartedly

Girl What is it, you know, you want to get?

Man A violin.

Girl A violin?

Man Yes, my old violin.

Girl Oh.

Man Have you never seen it?

Girl No.

Man She never showed it to you?

Girl Who?

Man My mother. She never showed it to you?

Girl When?

Man When you came round after school.

Girl To wait for my dad?

Man Yeah.

Girl And we listened to your records?

Man Yeah.

Girl No. Never.

Man Oh.

Girl I don't even know what it looks like.

Man Well, it's a violin; you know what a violin looks like.

Girl Yes, but not yours.

Man Well, mine's a violin like any other. Except it's mine. You sure you've never seen it?

Girl (*picking up the cup and saucer*) This must be cold now. I'll make you some more.

Man What? No, it doesn't matter.

Girl I'll wash it up, then.
Man Whatever.

The Girl exits into the kitchen with the cup and saucer

The Man continues searching

The Lights cross-fade to the "past" state

The Woman enters forty years ago. She no longer wears her pearl necklace

Woman It's no use your looking, Maurice, you'll not find it there.

The Man becomes his younger self, the Boy

Boy Where is it, then?

The Woman holds up the key. The Boy makes a grab for it and a short chase ensues

Woman A-a-a!
Boy I just want to know what it is.
Woman It's supposed to be for when you start at the Grammar.
Boy But the results aren't till next week.
Woman And you can't wait one little week?
Boy Please ...
Woman (*after a pause*) Oh, well, I don't suppose it'll hurt to let you
    see it. (*She goes to the cupboard and unlocks it*)
Boy Is it a bike?
Woman A bike? No, it's not a bike. How would I get a bike in here?
Boy I don't ... Is it a train?
Woman Now, what would you want with a train at your age? Trains
    are for little boys, not for young men who go to the Grammar.
Boy But we don't know yet if ——
Woman No, it's something better than a train or a bike; something
    very special; very precious.
Boy What is it?

Woman Hold out your hands.

The Boy does so

   And close your eyes.
Boy Aw!
Woman Come on!

The Woman goes into the cupboard then looks to check the Boy's still got his eyes closed. He hasn't, so he closes them. The Woman emerges with a violin case and lays it in the Boy's waiting arms

   There.

He opens his eyes. Pause

   Here. (*She opens the violin case*)

The Boy looks at the violin

Boy It's a violin.
Woman Your violin. (*Pause*) Well? Do you like it?
Boy I thought ——
Woman Beautiful, isn't it?
Boy I can't play it.
Woman Not yet. But we'll find you a teacher; get you lessons. And if you practise — practise very hard — who knows, you could end up giving concerts and making records like Yehudi Menuhin. Would you like that?
Boy I don't ——
Woman You can take it out, if you like — if your hands are clean; are your hands clean? (*She looks at his hands*) They'll do. Here, I'll hold the case.

The Woman holds the case; the Boy takes the violin from it

Boy It's dead light.
Woman (*handing him the bow*) Here.

The Boy takes the bow and stands, awkwardly

Now, let me have a look at you. Well, go on; hold it proper.

The Boy assumes a pose. He is ill at ease

Boy Like this?
Woman I know. Here ... (*She puts the record on*)

The music plays

Can you hear this, Maurice? Are you listening? This could be you.
If you practise. This could be you.
Boy I thought ——
Woman You'll be the only boy round here with his own violin.
Boy Yeah ...
Woman When I was your age ... (*She listens to the music: transfixed, transported*)
Boy Mum?
Woman (*coming to*) Mm? (*Beat*) We'll put it away now, shall we? (*She closes the case*) We'll put it away and keep it in here; keep it safe. (*She puts the violin and bow back in the case and the case in the cupboard which she locks. She turns off the record player and heads for the kitchen*) I'll get us some tea.
Boy Where's your necklace?
Woman (*pausing but not turning round*) Oh, don't you worry about that, Maurice. You just worry about passing for the Grammar.

The Woman exits

Boy (*after a moment, quietly*) I thought it was going to be a bike. (*He goes to the cupboard and kicks the door*)

The Lights return to the "present" state

The Girl enters. She stands and looks at the Man

Girl How d'you know it's even in there?

Man What?

Girl Your violin. I mean, you haven't been for ages — years and years — so how d'you know it's even in there?

Man Where else would it be? That's where it was always kept — so where else would it be?

Girl She might've sold it.

Man No.

Girl She might have given it away.

Man You don't know her.

Girl People change.

Man Is that right?

Girl I'm just saying it's been so long ——

Man All right, all right; you've made your point.

Girl Just saying.

Man Look, whose mother is she? This is my mum we're talking about, have you got that? Not some old woman who lives next door; my mum; my mother, OK? I think I might know what she'd do and what she wouldn't do, don't you, eh? Eh? (*He opens a drawer of the sideboard*) Oh, my God!

Girl What is it?

Man I don't believe ... She must've kept them!

Girl What?

Pause. The Man takes a red and white scarf, bobble hat and wooden football rattle from the drawer. He sounds the rattle and laughs

(*Covering her ears*) What's that?

Man (*stopping laughing*) This? This is an official Man U rattle, scarf and bobble hat, complete — please note — with the actual portraits of the actual players: Alex Stepney; Nobby Stiles; Pat Crerand.

Girl Who?

Man You got them with the programmes ... I think you ... (*Pause*) God, must be, what? ... '65? '66?

Girl The Swinging Sixties.

Man Ha!
Girl We did it in History.
Man History? That's my life you're talking about.
Girl You must be dead old, then.
Man I'm not old.
Girl You're bald.
Man Yeah, well; some men go bald in their twenties.
Girl You're not in your twenties.
Man No, all right.
Girl (*after a moment*) So, were they?
Man What?
Girl The Sixties: swinging.
Man Not that I remember. Not in this house. Flapping ... Dripping ...
Girl How d'you mean?
Man She was always washing, wringing, scrubbing — up to her elbows in the twin tub.

The Woman enters with a scrubbing brush; she kneels and cleans the floor in front of the kitchen door

Girl The what?
Man It was like a washing machine; was a washing machine ...
Man ⎫
Woman ⎭ (*together*) *All washing and no machine.*
Girl She used to do ours.
Man Your washing?
Girl Yeah. Before my dad ... Before we got one of our own, your ... Mrs Metcalf used to do our sheets and that. Said she didn't like to see a fella going to the launderette.
Man Never one for dirty linen in public, Mum.
Girl And my dad, right, he'd do her a shop once a week. Cos you can get things cheaper at the big ASDA but it's down the Stockport road.
Man Where the hospital used to be.
Girl Dunno. Best bargain-hunter in town, my dad.
Man That right?

Girl That's what your … What Mrs Metcalf says.
Man And her hands ...
Girl You what?
Man My mum: her hands.
Girl What about them?
Man Red. And the smell ...
Girl They don't smell.
Man Vim.
Girl What?
Man It was a powder — scouring powder — you know, for cleaning.
Girl Cleaning what?
Man Anything. Everything. The sink; the back step; my knees. So her hands were red, always red. But they smelled white. Red and white ... And she used to iron my shorts. Iron them: my football shorts.
Girl Is that bad?
Man I'd throw them on the ground on the way to school; jump on them.
Girl Why?
Man No-one else had their shorts ironed.
Girl So?
Man So things were bad enough without her carrying on like we're better than everyone else. It's like this. (*He sounds the rattle*)

The Woman looks up from her work and exits

She hated all this. Every Saturday — and if they were playing away, we'd watch the Reserves. Hated it. (*After a moment*) So did I.
Girl What!?
Man Oh, I never told her; never said. Standing on the terraces, freezing your … Freezing to death; blokes in front so you can't see what was going on ...
Girl Then why did you go?
Man It was what you did, I suppose. What everybody did. What I did — to be one of the crowd; in with the in-crowd.

Girl But why?
Man So I wouldn't just be Maurice Metcalf: the skinny kid with the
   violin.
Girl Were you skinny?
Man Pretty much.
Girl And is that your real name: Maurice?
Man What?
Girl Maurice: is that your real name?
Man Yes.
Girl I can see why you changed it.

The Man sounds the rattle

Man I wonder why she kept it.
Girl (*beat*) Yeah.

The Man returns to the cupboard door and tries it again

   Someone might've taken it. Your violin. A thief or someone.
Man (*beat*) Then why is the door locked?
Girl I don't know.
Man She kept it locked cos that's where she kept the violin. You're
   not looking very hard, are you?
Girl Why d'you need it, anyway?
Man What? Well, I ... I need to practise, don't I?
Girl Do you?
Man Course I do. You have to practise every day.
Girl Even now?
Man Yes.
Girl (*beat*) But where's your other one?
Man Other what?
Girl Your other violin; the one you give your concerts on?
Man Oh, right ...
Girl And make your records with.
Man Oh, that.
Girl Your Stradivarius.
Man My Stradivarius ... Yeah, well, I left New Zealand in such a
   hurry, I forgot it.

Girl Oh. Right. What's it like?
Man (*trying the cupboard door again*) What?
Girl New Zealand.
Man Oh, it's, er ... It's very nice.
Girl But is it hot or cold or what?
Man Oh, I see ... Well, it varies.
Girl And what's your house like?
Man Look, I thought you did it in Geography. (*Pause*) Damn. I
    wonder if ...

The Man heads for the kitchen door

Girl Where you going?

   The Man doesn't answer; he exits

*Alone, the Girl hesitates then produces the cupboard key and looks
at it. She leaves it in a variety of locations. From the kitchen come
the sounds of the Man's return. The Girl panics and puts the key
away*

   The Man enters with a screwdriver

Girl What you doing?
Man What's it look like? (*He tries to open the lock with the
    screwdriver*)
Girl (*alarmed*) Oh!
Man What?
Girl Nothing.

He looks at her and carries on

   Maybe you should just go.
Man Where?
Girl To the hospital; see your ... Mrs Metcalf. Maybe you should
    just go.
Man And maybe you should just mind your own business.
Girl (*after a pause*) I went last week.

Man Good for you.

Girl And my nan went yesterday.

Man And I expect your dad'll be going tomorrow.

Girl My ... I don't know. Only my nan says it won't be long.

Man What won't?

Girl You know, before your ... Mrs Metcalf ... Before she ...

Man (*beat*) Yeah, well, she's very old.

Girl My nan says she's no age.

Man She says a lot, your nan, doesn't she?

Girl Yeah, and she says ...

Man What?

Girl (*beat*) Nothing.

Man Come on, what?

Girl (*after a pause*) She says it's a disgrace you've not been to see your mum for so long.

Man Is that right?

Girl And that when you think of everything your mum did for you, what sort of son can you be?

Man She says that.

Girl But I told her it wasn't your fault; that you'd got commitments and that and concert schedules and recording sessions and you can't just drop everything and fly halfway round the world at the drop of a hat and that anyway your mum didn't mind because she knows how busy you are.

Man Yeah, that's right.

Girl So if you want to go — to the hospital, you know — just go.

Man I told you; I need to get my violin. (*Struggling with the lock*) Bloody thing. Bloody, bloody thing.

Girl I don't think you should swear like that.

Man Why, who are you, Mother Teresa?

Girl Who? No, I mean, I don't think your ... Mrs Metcalf would like it.

Man Oh, you don't?

Girl She doesn't like ——

Man You're quite the little expert, aren't you, where my mum's concerned?

Girl I only meant ... (*Pause*) Do you want me to have another look upstairs?

Man Please yourself.

The Girl goes up the stairs, pausing to take the key from her pocket and look back at the Man. She exits

The Man tries to unscrew the hinges on the cupboard door but they won't budge

The Lights cross-fade to the "past" setting

Woman (*off*) It's only me.

The Woman enters, forty years ago, straight from work

Oh, there you are. Have you done it, then?

The Man becomes the Boy

Boy Think so. It was the hinges. They'd got a bit loose so the door'd dropped and that's why it was sticking.
Woman Is that right?
Boy Yeah.
Woman (*inspecting his work*) And where did you learn all this?
Boy We did it in woodwork.
Woman I see. They do teach you something at that school, then.
Boy Can I go now?
Woman Where?
Boy It's Saturday.
Woman You don't say: been rushed off our feet this morning in the shop.
Boy (*putting on the bobble hat*) There's a match.
Woman Have you done your practice? (*Pause*) Well, have you? (*Pause*) Maurice, I'm talking to you.
Boy Yes.
Woman What does that mean?
Boy I've done it, yes.
Woman Let me hear you, then.
Boy What?

Woman What you've been practising.

Boy I've done it.

Woman Yes, and I want to hear you. (*Pause*) Did you do your practice, Maurice? (*Pause*) Did you? (*Pause*) You know the rules.

Boy Your rules.

Woman My rules, that's right. My house, my rules.

Boy It's not fair!

Woman Not fair? Do you think life's fair, Maurice? Do you? If life was fair I wouldn't be working every hour God sends. If life was fair, you'd be at the Grammar. If life was fair your father'd be here — and we'd all be telling a different story. (*Beat*) Now do your practice.

Boy I don't want to.

Woman Well, we can't always do what we want.

Boy I don't even like it.

Woman And I don't like you going to the match as you call it.

Boy That's what it is.

Woman Mucking and messing about is what it is.

Boy Yeah, with my friends.

Woman A bunch of dead-legs who could all do with a damn good wash and some decent manners if you ask me.

Boy Well, no-one did.

Woman And that's enough of that. (*Pause*) I don't know, Maurice. If only you'd passed for the Grammar.

Boy Well, I didn't. Will you stop going on about it?

Woman As if you didn't see enough of them at school without mixing with them weekends.

Boy Who?

Woman You know who I mean.

Boy No. Who?

Woman Them from the flats.

Boy Oh, the flats! Shock, horror!

Woman Yes, the flats.

Boy It's where they live, not who they are.

Woman It's what they're like. That Jimmy O'Rourke: I've never seen him but he's not kicking a ball.

Boy He's got a trial for United.

Woman Oh honestly, Maurice, I think we might set our sights a bit higher than that, don't you?

Boy You're not the Queen, you know.

Woman (*after a beat*) I beg your pardon?

Boy You carry on like you were the Queen or summat.

Woman Something.

Boy Well, you're not. This is just a council house; you just work in a shop.

Woman You don't have to tell me, Maurice. I know where I work. And I know why: because I want you to have a decent home to come home to with decent food on the table and the chance to grow up and make something of yourself. And what you look like in that hat, I don't know.

Boy Everyone else wears one.

Woman Do they? And if everyone else wore a plant-pot on their head, I suppose you'd do the same?

Boy No.

Woman I'm glad to hear it.

Boy I just want to go to the match.

Woman Well, you're going nowhere till you've done your practice.

Boy Aw!

Woman You're all right, you've hours to kick-off or whatever you call it.

Boy No, we're meeting early so we can ...

Woman So you can what?

Boy Nothing.

Woman So you can muck about down by the docks again? Well, you can forget it. That Jimmy O'Rourke and his pals can do what they like but I don't want you involved. It'll be the police next. Oh, yes, I know all about it; heard all about it; was told all about it by that Mrs Fisher from the church. Her husband saw you, apparently. I said, I'm sure it wasn't my lad. But no, he was very particular, she said: the boy with the violin. Now let me hear you doing your practice for half an hour while I do the sheets and then you can go to the match. But I want you straight back here for your tea.

The Woman exits

The Lights cross-fade to the "present" state

The Man takes off the football regalia. Pause. The Man's mobile phone rings

> *The Girl enters from upstairs, the cupboard key in her hand; she hovers on the stairs, overhearing the following*

Man (*answering the phone*) Hallo? ... Yeah. ... Yeah, look, I told you already. ... Yeah, that's right. ... No, I'm not. ... Look, what is it with you?... Yeah, all right, I didn't mean ... Yeah, I will. ... Yeah. ... I know, yeah.

There is a pause. The Man stares at his phone

Girl (*coming into the room*) Who was that?
Man (*going to the cupboard*) No-one.
Girl No-one?

The Man tries the cupboard door ever more urgently

You need it really bad, then?
Man I told you; I've got to practise.
Girl Can't you just miss one day?
Man No.
Girl But why?
Man (*after a beat*) I've got a concert, haven't I?
Girl Really?
Man Yes, really.
Girl Where is it?
Man What?
Girl The concert. Where's it going to be?
Man Er ... The Albert Hall.
Girl In London?
Man Yes.
Girl I went there with my dad.

Man Really.

Girl We went to see *The Lion King* — not the film, I'd seen the film, the play, the musical — and we went on a boat and we had our tea at Planet Hollywood and we were going to go on the London Eye, you know, the wheel thing, only it was closed or something and can I come?

Man What?

Girl To your concert. Can I?

Man Well ...

Girl Please!

Man I don't ——

Girl What are you going to play?

Man When?

Girl What are you going to play at your concert?

Man Oh ... I haven't decided.

Girl Haven't you?

Man No.

Girl Your ... Mrs Metcalf says you have to be able to play loads of pieces off by heart so that you can do whatever they ask you.

Man Yeah, that's right.

Girl (*going through the records*) So you could play this ... Or this ... Or this! Oh, yes: play this; play this! (*She puts the record on*)

The music plays

The Woman enters, forty years ago, pausing in her work to listen

Girl Will you? Will you play this?

Man Er ... Yeah. Yeah, I might.

Girl Might?

Man Will, then.

Girl I'll bet you're glad you learnt, eh?

Man What?

Girl I'll bet you're glad you practised, cos now you get to go all over the world giving concerts and being famous.

Man Yeah, well ...

Girl Oh, please can I come?

Man It's too far.

Girl No, I've been.
Man I'm sure your dad would think it was too far.
Girl No, he came with me.
Man And where is he, anyway?
Girl Who?
Man Your dad: where is he? Eh?
Girl Oh, he'll be here in a bit.
Man You keep saying that.
Girl He must be late. Oh, listen to this bit: listen to this! (*She turns up the volume*)
Woman Can you hear this, Maurice? Are you listening? This could be you. If you practise. This could be you.

The Woman exits

The Man turns the music off. Pause

Girl Is it really good enough to play at a concert?
Man What?
Girl Your violin.
Man Yeah.
Girl So, it's worth loads of money, then?
Man It better be.
Girl I didn't know.

The Man gives the Girl a sudden, searching look

I mean, when you see it ——
Man I thought you hadn't seen it.
Girl I haven't.
Man But you just said ——
Girl No. I haven't, honest. (*She puts her hand behind her back*)
Man What's that you've got?
Girl Nothing.
Man Is that the key?
Girl No.
Man What is it, then?

Girl Nothing.
Man If it's the key ——
Girl It isn't.
Man Show me, then. Show me.

*The Girl dodges the Man and puts the key in her mouth. He catches
her and turns her round to face him*

Let me see what's in your hand.

The Girl holds out her empty hand

And the other one.

She does so

Man Where is it?

Unable to open her mouth, the Girl fails to answer

The key. Where is it?

The Girl pulls a face as if to say she doesn't know

Well?

The Girl freezes, not knowing how to proceed

Man Open your mouth. (*Beat*) Now.

The Girl does so

Tongue.

She sticks out her tongue. There is the key

Thank you.

She gives him the key. He turns to the cupboard and makes to unlock it

Girl My dad went to school with you.
Man (*stopping short*) What?
Girl My dad. He went to school with you.
Man Your dad?
Girl Yeah.
Man You sure?
Girl He says he did.
Man What's he called?
Girl Jimmy.
Man Not ——
Girl O'Rourke.
Man Jimmy O'Rourke?
Girl Yeah.
Man Your dad?
Girl Yeah.
Man Jimmy O'Rourke!
Girl It's true, then?
Man Yeah.
Girl And you remember him?
Man Remember?
Girl He remembers you.
Man I'll bet. Yeah, well, I was well known, you see: my mother saw to that.
Girl How?
Man The violin.
Girl Didn't you want that?
Man I wanted to be like your dad.
Girl My dad?
Man I used to go to football with him; watch United. Well, I used to tag along.
Girl The Stretford End.
Man That's right. Not that my mother knew that bit. He could play an' all.
Girl Football mad, my nan says.

Man Dribbling; passing; in the air ... As far was I was concerned,
    he walked on water.
Girl I thought you didn't like football.
Man I didn't like being different.
Girl (*after a pause*) He had a trial, you know, for United.
Man That's right, he did. So where is he now?
Girl What?
Man What did he end up doing?
Girl Oh, he was a ... He's a copper.
Man What? Your dad, a copper?
Girl Yeah.
Man Jimmy O'Rourke?
Girl Yeah.

Pause. The Man turns again to the cupboard

    And you know something else?
Man Not now. (*He opens the cupboard door*)
Girl I mean, don't you think you should go to the hospital first?

*The Man enters the cupboard. After a moment the Girl makes for the
door to the hallway. The Man emerges from the cupboard with the
violin case*

Man Where you going?
Girl Nowhere.
Man I thought you were waiting for your dad.
Girl I am.
Man Well, then? (*He makes to open the case*)
Girl (*running to the record player*) Here, listen to this.
Man Not now.

The Man opens the violin case. It is empty. Pause

Man OK. Where is it?
Girl What?
Man Don't play games, kid.

Girl I'm not.

Man I haven't got time for games.

Girl I don't know what you mean.

Man Look, if you know where it is, just tell me.

Girl I don't.

Man No?

Girl No.

Man I don't think you're telling me the truth, are you?

Girl About what?

Man About the violin, what do you think?

Girl I am.

Man You lied about the key.

Girl I——

Man Look, I need that violin.

Girl Can't you borrow one?

Man What?

Girl For the concert.

Man What?

Girl The concert.

Man Look, there is no concert.

Girl What do you mean?

Man There is no concert. There are no concerts. There never were any concerts. No concerts; no records; nothing.

Girl (*beat*) You're not Yehudi Menuhin, then?

Man No.

Girl No. (*Pause*) I saw it on the news when he died the other year and they never mentioned him coming from round here. And your … Mrs Metcalf never said; just went on talking about you.

Man (*after a moment*) Why didn't you say?

Girl It was a good story.

Man Right.

Girl (*after a time*) So you don't live in New Zealand?

Man No.

Girl Then where've you been all these years?

Man Southampton. (*Beat*) Prison.

Girl (*after a time*) Did you kill someone?

Man Don't be ... No. No, nothing like that.

Girl What then?

Man Fraud. You know: pretending to be someone you're not.

Girl Were you pretending to be Yehudi Menuhin?

Man No, that was just what my mother wanted to believe. There's no law against that. No, I was pretending to be someone with lots of money so I could get my hands on some for real.

Girl Don't understand.

Man If you've got nothing, you get nothing; but if you've got, you get more. It's the way of the world, kid.

Girl And what did you want to get?

Man Something right for once. I dunno.

Girl (*after a time*) What was it like? You know, in prison?

Man Scary. Then you get used to it. But it's like you're not really a person. That's the hardest bit: staying a person.

Girl And did she never come and see you, Mrs … Your mum?

Man It was me. I didn't want her to.

Pause

Girl Do you play the violin even a bit?

Man I shouldn't think so after all these years. I was never much cop.

Girl Then why do you need it?

Man To sell.

Girl Sell?

Man I'm in trouble and I need the money.

Girl What for?

Man I owe people.

Girl Can't they wait?

Man They're not the sort of people who like to be kept waiting.

Girl Is that who you were talking to on the phone?

Man Yes.

Girl What will happen if you don't pay them?

Man They'll hurt me.

Girl Badly?

Man Yes.

The Girl exits

Where you going now?

The Man closes the empty violin case and returns to the cupboard, emerging with a music stand and a score. He turns the pages of the music

The Lights cross-fade to the "past" state

The Woman enters, forty years ago

The Man becomes the Boy

Woman So, have you decided?
Boy What?
Woman What you want to do for your birthday?
Boy Don't mind.
Woman Would you like something special for your tea?
Boy Don't mind.
Woman Shall I make a trifle? Or you can have fish fingers.
Boy Don't mind.
Woman Thirteen! A teenager! You can have a friend round if you
    want.
Boy Can Jimmy come?
Woman Jimmy O'Rourke?
Boy Yeah.
Woman Oh, I'm not sure about that, Maurice.
Boy What does that mean?
Woman It means, look what happened the last time he came.
Boy It was an accident.
Woman It was a new window in the back room was what it was.
Boy It was me, I told you.
Woman I don't care who it was, it was while he was here.
Boy It's my birthday.

Pause

Woman Or we could go into town, how about that? Have our tea somewhere nice — St Ann's Square way — the Kardomah or Meng and Eckker's. (*Pause*) Or we could go to that Wimpy Bar: you'd like that.

Boy Don't mind.

Woman (*after a pause*) And then on the Saturday I've got something special planned.

Boy What?

Woman (*after a beat*) It was going to be a surprise, but I don't suppose it matters.

Boy What is it?

Woman You and me, we're going to get on a train to London — and we can have our dinner on the train and everything, you know, in the dining-car — and then when we get there we're going to go on the underground train — I've got it written down, the woman in the travel agents wrote it all down for me — and I've got us two tickets for a concert at the Royal Albert Hall.

Boy What?

Woman Yehudi Menuhin.

Boy On Saturday?

Woman And then afterwards we're going to come back on the sleeper — you know the train you can sleep on — they have little bunk beds apparently but it's quite private ... So what do you say to that?

Boy (*after a time*) There's a match.

Woman Well, I think this is a bit more exciting than a match, don't you, Maurice?

Boy It's a Cup-tie.

Woman Oh, well, if it's Cup-tie!

Boy Quarter-final. Everyone's going.

Woman And you'd rather go to watch football than hear Yehudi Menuhin?

Boy Isn't he playing any other night?

Woman Oh, I expect so, Maurice. I expect he's playing in New York or Paris or ... Would you like me to get tickets for those?

Boy I didn't mean ——

Woman This was going to be our special treat but of course, if
you've got other plans ...

Boy No.

Woman Well, that's what it sounds like. You know who this is,
Maurice? You know who I'm talking about? This is Yehudi
Menuhin. Yehudi Menuhin.

Boy Don't even like Yehudi Menuhin.

Woman You've never heard him!

Boy I've heard his records.

Woman What does ——?

Boy He plays the violin, doesn't he?

Woman You know full well ——

Boy Then why would I like him if he plays the violin?

Woman Now you're being silly.

Boy No. It's you; you're the one who likes it; you, not me.

Woman That's not ——

Boy You're the one who wanted me to have the thing in the first
place; to practise; have lessons; be different from everyone else
— well, I don't want it; don't want to be different; don't want your
lessons or your records or your bloody violin.

Woman (*after a beat*) Do you know what it's cost me for you to
have that violin?

Boy You can sell it for all I care; you can give it away. I don't want
it; I never wanted it to start with and I never want to see it again.

Woman You don't mean that, Maurice.

Boy I do. I do mean it.

Pause

Woman Ask him, then. Jimmy Whatsisname. Ask him if you want
to.

Boy No.

Woman Then don't ask him.

Boy I asked him already.

Woman So what are you going on about?

Boy He said no. Said he didn't want to. Said I was a snob and a creep.
And it's your fault. Your fault. And I hate you! (*He knocks over
the music stand and runs up the stairs but stops halfway in tears*)

Pause

The Woman slowly rights the music stand and replaces the music. She turns to go into the kitchen. She starts to cry. Mother and son cry, each unseen by the other

The Girl appears in the doorway with the violin

The Woman exits

The Lights cross-fade to the "present" state

The Girl goes over to the Man and holds the violin out to him. He comes down the stairs, looks at her and takes the violin. He looks at it for a long time

Girl I took it.
Man Right.
Girl After Mrs ... After your mum went into hospital.
Man I see.
Girl There's nothing wrong with it. I didn't do anything. Just took it home. (*After a time*) Play it. (*Pause*) Please.

The Man takes the violin, goes to the music stand and tunes up, but falters and turns away. Then something happens. There is applause

The Lights cross-fade to a state suggesting a concert hall

The Woman enters

The Man turns and sees his mother. An orchestra comes in. He's on the platform at the Royal Albert Hall: playing. The concerto reaches its breathless conclusion. There is thunderous applause

The Woman exits

The Lights return to the "present" state

Pause

Girl I wish I could play.
Man Maybe if you ask your dad ——
Girl No.
Man You never know. I'll have a word if you like.
Girl You're not mad with me, then?
Man No. Not now. No. He can't be long now, can he? (*Pause*)
    I said ——
Girl He's not coming.
Man How do you mean?
Girl My dad: he's not coming.
Man But ——
Girl He's dead.
Man (*beat*) I thought you were waiting for him; thought that's what
    you were doing here in the first place.
Girl It was. Is.
Man Is anything you've told me the truth?

Pause

Girl It was a year ago. Nearly a year. It was after school so I was
    here, you know, waiting for my dad to get back from work. And
    your mum was here too and I made her a coffee in the china cup
    and she'd told me what you'd said in your last letter: how you
    were coming to see her soon. And she put on one of your records
    — this record — and we were just listening to the music and I was
    pretending, cos sometimes I did, that it was me playing and not
    you ——
Man It wasn't me.
Girl No. I know, but, anyway, it wasn't me, was it? And my dad was
    really late but I didn't care cos your mum sent me upstairs for the
    key, you know to the cupboard, and she fetched it out, the violin,
    and let me see it; touch it; let me take it out and hold it; feel it ...

It's dead light ... So I'm playing, like, pretending — and remembering — I think it was a memory or a dream ——

The Lights cross-fade to a dreamlike state

— it could've been, but anyway, we're on a beach — this is my dad and me — it's warm and yellow and we're playing football — scoring goals at Wembley and the ball gets blown away and we go running after it and laughing down towards the water hand in hand and suddenly he picks me up; he scoops me up; he lifts me at the water's edge and swings me out above the waves: I'm flying — safe and screaming — beaming, roaring, soaring where the yellow meets the sea ...

The Lights snap back to the "present" setting

(*Beat*) And then there's a knock at the door. And it's my nan. It's not my dad; it's my nan. And I knew straight away. Nobody said anything — not a word — but I knew. And then they were speaking; looking at me; speaking but I couldn't hear them. Only the music. And I couldn't let go. Of the violin, you know. My nan had to bend my fingers for your mum to take it off me. (*Pause*) I didn't tell people. At school and that. People knew, I think, but I didn't tell 'em; didn't want to talk about it; didn't want ... (*Pause*) We've still got his things: his clothes and that. They're in the wardrobe in my nan's room — well, it's my nan's room now — and sometimes I go and sit in there. In the wardrobe. Do you think that's mad?

Man No.

Girl Or sometimes, on a Saturday and that, I play hide and seek like we used to and I hide — cos he was always It — and he never finds me or if I'm doing a Pot Noodle to sit and watch telly with, I do Spicy Beef even though I don't really like Spicy Beef, cos that was his favourite ... Pretending. (*Pause*) This is his coat. His jacket. I wear it. All the time. Don't take it off. Even in bed.

Man What about at school?

Girl No.

Man What about when it's games?

Girl Bunk off. Come here; sit with your mum. Listen to the record. And after school I kept on coming. And I kept on coming even when she wasn't there, your mum; even when she went to hospital. Like I was still waiting for him. Like he was still going to come home.

Man (*after a moment*) Jimmy O'Rourke.

Girl Yeah.

Pause. He holds out the violin. She looks at him

Man Here. My mother would want you to have it.

She takes the violin and looks at it. Pause. The Man's mobile phone rings. He takes it out and looks at it. The Girl looks at him then holds out the violin

Girl Your mother would want you to sell it.

Man No.

Girl She would.

The Woman enters

Woman Can you hear this, Maurice? Are you listening?

Man But what about ——

Girl Sometimes it's good to pretend. And sometimes it's good to stop.

The Man turns off his phone without answering. The Girl takes down the hood of her coat. He takes the violin and puts it in the case. She takes off her coat

Girl What are you going to do now?

The Woman picks up the Man's coat and holds it out to him. The Man takes it

Man Go to the hospital. Say good-bye. What about you?
Girl (*picking up the metal polish*) I'll just put this away. Then I'd
better go. Get my things ready. It's games tomorrow.

The Girl exits to the kitchen

*The Man takes the violin, takes a last look at the room and exits,
watched by the Woman*

*The Girl enters, decides to leave the coat and exits, watched by the
Woman*

Violin music plays

*The Woman, alone now, picks up the football regalia; folds it; then
holds it to her breast*

The house fades away to Black-out

The music finishes

FURNITURE AND PROPERTY LIST

On stage: Hallstand
Sideboard. *On it*: brass candlesticks. *In it*: scarf, bobble hat, wooden football rattle
Easy chair
Record player
Records without outer sleeves

Off stage: Bedding (**Woman**)
Tin of metal polish (Duraglit) (**Girl**)
Pile of clean sheets (**Woman**)
Cup of coffee on saucer (**Girl**)
Box, china cups, newspaper (**Woman**)
Key to cupboard door (**Woman**)
Violin and bow in case (**Woman**)
Scrubbing brush (**Woman**)
Screwdriver (**Man**)
Music stand and score (**Man**)

Personal: **Woman**: pearl necklace
Man: mobile phone

LIGHTING PLOT

Practical fittings required: nil
One interior. The same throughout

To open: Dim afternoon light

Cue 1	The **Girl** puts on the light *Snap on overhead room lights*	(Page 2)
Cue 2	The **Man** pauses by the record player *Cross-fade to "past" state*	(Page 6)
Cue 3	The **Boy** looks at the record player *Cross-fade to "present" state*	(Page 9)
Cue 4	The **Girl** turns the volume up *Cross-fade to dreamlike setting*	(Page 14)
Cue 5	The **Man** turns the music off *Cross-fade lights to "present" state*	(Page 14)
Cue 6	The **Girl** exits; the **Man** continues searching *Cross-fade to "past" state*	(Page 16)
Cue 7	The **Boy** goes to the cupboard and kicks the door *Cross-fade to "present" state*	(Page 18)
Cue 8	The **Man** tries to unscrew the hinges *Cross-fade to "past" state*	(Page 25)
Cue 9	*The* **Woman** *exits* *Cross-fade to "present" state*	(Page 28)

Cue 10   The **Man** turns the pages of the music   (Page 36)
Cross-fade to "past" state

Cue 11   The **Woman** exits   (Page 39)
Cross-fade to "present" state

Cue 12   Applause   (Page 39)
Cross-fade to "concert hall" lighting

Cue 13   The **Woman** exits   (Page 39)
Cross-fade to "present" state

Cue 14   **Girl**: " ... a memory or a dream ——"   (Page 41)
Cross-fade to dreamlike state

Cue 15   **Girl**: " ... where the yellow meets the sea ..."   (Page 41)
Snap back to "present" state

Cue 16   The **Woman** holds the football regalia to her breast (Page 43)
Fade to black-out

EFFECTS PLOT

www.ingramcontent.com/pod-product-compliance
Ingram Content Group UK Ltd.
Pitfield, Milton Keynes, MK11 3LW, UK
UKHW021822150726
7214IPUK00017B/270